Aldine Silliman Kieffer

Sharon's Dewy Rose

A Collection of New Music and Hymns for the Use of Sabbath-Schools

Aldine Silliman Kieffer

Sharon's Dewy Rose
A Collection of New Music and Hymns for the Use of Sabbath-Schools

ISBN/EAN: 9783337420055

Printed in Europe, USA, Canada, Australia, Japan

Cover: Foto ©Thomas Meinert / pixelio.de

More available books at **www.hansebooks.com**

SHARON'S DEWY ROSE.

→:A COLLECTION:←

OF

NEW MUSIC AND HYMNS

FOR THE USE OF

Sabbath-schools, Prayer Meetings, and Special Occasions.

BY

ALDINE S. KIEFFER and J. H. TENNEY.

RUEBUSH, KIEFFER & CO.,

Music Publishers:

DAYTON, ROCKINGHAM CO., VIRGINIA.

1880.

PREFATORY NOTE.

THE increasing demand for new music printed in seven character notes, accounts for the authors and publishers having prepared this new volume for use in Sabbath-schools. They desire to call particular attention to the following hymns and tunes:—

✵THE SCALE.✵

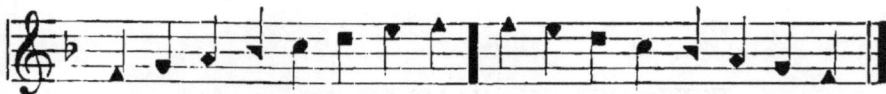

Doe, Ray, Mee, Faw, Sole, Law, See, Doe.   Doe, See, Law, Sole, Faw, Mee, Ray, Doe.

J. M. ARMSTRONG & CO., MUSIC TYPOGRAPHERS, Philadelphia.

SHARON'S DEWY ROSE.

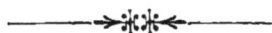

SHARON'S DEWY ROSE.

Rev. J. B. ATCHINSON.

Duet or Quartette.

1 O Dew of heav-en, fall Up - on this Rose! May it a bless-ing prove,
2 O Light of heav-en, shine, And beau-ti - fy The path of these song flowers,
3 O Ho - ly Spir - it, breathe Up - on this flower! In - spire this Dew-y Rose,
4 Go, Sharon's Dew - y Rose, Go forth to bless! Go teach the mul-ti - tudes

CHORUS.

Wher - e'er it goes!
Wher - e'er they fly!
And give it power! } O Christ, thou Rose of Sha - ron, This Rose we of - fer
Of hap-pi - ness!

thee: May this "Song-Rose of Sha - ron" Draw mul - ti - tudes to thee!

3

Mrs. E. W. CHAPMAN.   # A CUP OF WATER.   *

1 Pass-ing thro' this world of sor-row, This true pleas-ure we may claim;
2 Wea-ry hearts with sor-row weep-ing, We may guide in heav-en's road,
3 We may com-fort those a-wea-ry; Make the home a cheer-ful place;

Oft to give a cup of wa-ter, In the Sa-viour's prec-ious name:
Cheer-ful words, and ten-der, speak-ing In the name of Christ our Lord;
Give to all a hand of help-ing; Wear for all a smil-ing face;

Help and hap-pi-ness be-stow-ing, For the sake of Cal-vary's Lord,
We may give the cup of wa-ter To some thirs-ty, fam-ished soul.
Rays of God's bright sun-shine spreading In the storm-y way of pain,

That we may re-ceive the bless-ing, And in-her-it the re-ward.
Wipe a-way the crys-tal tear-drops, Or the storm of grief con-trol.
Till in yon-der world of glo-ry We the crown of life shall gain.

A CUP OF WATER.

Though it be an hum-ble ser-vice, But a cup of wa-ter pure,

If 'tis done for love of Je-sus, The re-ward is ev-er sure.

MAXEY.

J. McP.

JOHN McPHERSON.

1 Raise we now our morn-ing song, To our King whose love we own,
2 Thro' the sol-emn hours of night, He has watched with ten-der care,
3 In the fu-ture He will guide Till we reach a shore so sweet,

Glad we meet in hap-py throng, And sur-round this earth-ly throne.
Bid us greet the morn-ing light, And the day beams bright and fair.
Where the streams of bliss will glide, And our friends a-gain we'll meet.

5

WAITING.

1 I am wait-ing by the riv-er, And my heart has wait-ed long;
2 Far a-way be-yond the sha-dow Of this wea-ry vale of tears,
3 They are launching on the riv-er, From the calm and qui-et shore,

Now I think I hear the chor-us Of the an-gels' wel-come song:
There the tide of bliss is sweep-ing Thro' the bright and changeless years:
And they soon will bear my spir-it Where the wea-ry sigh no more:

Oh, I see the dawn is break-ing On the hill-tops of the blest!
Oh, I long to be with Je-sus, In the man-sions of the blest!
For the tide is swift-ly flow-ing, And I long to greet the blest,

Where the wick-ed cease from troubling, And the wea-ry are at rest,

WAITING.

Where the wick-ed cease from troubling, And the wea-ry are at rest. . . .

at rest.

MEDITATION.

A. S. KIEFFER.

1 As o'er the past my mem'-ry strays, Why heaves the se-cret sigh?
2 The world and world-ly things beloved, My anxious thoughts em-ployed;
· 3 Yet, Ho-ly Fa-ther, wild de-spair Chase from my la-b'ring breast;
4 My life's brief rem-nant all be thine And when thy sure de-cree

'Tis that I mourn de-part-ed days, Yet un-pre-pared to die.
And time un-hall-owed, un-improved, Pre-sents a fear-ful void.
Thy grace it ' is which prompts the prayer; That grace can do the rest.
Bids me this fleet-ing breath re-sign, Oh, speed my soul to thee!

1 My soul, come meditate the day,
    And think how near it stands,
When thou must quit this house of clay,
    And fly to unknown lands.

2 Oh, could we die with those that die,
    And place us in their stead,
Then would our spirits learn to fly,
    And converse with the dead:

3 Then we should see the saints above
    In their own glorious forms,
And wonder why our souls should love
    To dwell with mortal worms.

4 We should almost forsake our clay
    Before the summons come,
And pray, and wish our souls away,
    To their eternal home.

7

SINGING IN HEAVEN.

Gentle and slow.

A. S. KIEFFER.

1 'Tis pleas-ant to sing the sweet praise of our King, As
2 'Tis sweet to re-cline on thy bos-om di-vine, And
3 On Ca-nan's fair land we in tri-umph shall stand, With

here in this val-ley of sor-rows we rove; 'Twill be
feel that our hearts and our spir-its are thine; And, up-
crowns on our heads and with harps in our hands; While our

pleas-ant-er still when on Zi-on's fair hill We shall
held by thy love, we are blest from a-bove, As with
songs shall a-bound to the Lamb who is crowned, And ho-

CHORUS.

sing the sweet prais-es of Je-sus, a-bove. } Sing - ing in
sing-ing and tri-umph to Zi-on we move. }
san-nas to Je-sus through heav'n shall resound. } Singing with seraphs and

8

SINGING IN HEAVEN.

heav - en, yes, sing - ing in heav - en,
sing-ing in heav'n, Yes, sing-ing with ser - aphs and sing-ing in heav'n;

Oh, 'twill be sweet - er our sing - ing in heaven.
Oh, 'twill be sweet-er our singing in heav'n, Our sing - ing in heav'n.

SOMERVILLE.

A. S. KIEFFER.

1 Dear Je - sus, ev - er at my side, How lov - ing must thou be,
2 I can - not feel thee touch my hand, With pres- sure light and mild,
3 But I have felt thee in my thoughts, Re - buk - ing sin for me,
4 And when, dear Sa - viour, I kneel down Morn - ing and night to prayer,

To leave thy home in heav'n to guard A lit - tle child like me.
To check me as my moth - er did When I was but a child.
And when my heart loves God, I know The sweet-ness is from thee.
Some- thing there is with - in my heart Which tells me thou art there.

9

GUIDE ME, BLESSED SAVIOUR.

B. A. GLENN.

CHAS. EDW. POLLOCK, by per.

1 Guide me, oh, my bless-ed Sa-viour, For I need thee ev'-ry day;
2 Take me, oh, my Sa-viour, take me, Keep me ev - er near thy side;
3 All to thee I would sur - ren-der, Take me now, I hum-bly pray;

Leave me not a - lone to wan-der, Lest from thee I go a - stray.
All my hope is firm-ly anchored, On the cross where thou hast died.
Guide me through this world of dark-ness, To the light of end-less day.

CHORUS.

Guide me, oh, my blessed Sa-viour, For I need thee ev'-ry hour;
Guide me, oh, my blessed Sa-viour, For I need thee ev'ry hour;

Through my tri - als be thou near me, And up - hold me with thy pow'r.
Through my tri-als be thou near me, And uphold me with thy pow'r.

PRECIOUS SPIRIT!

Mrs. E. C. ELLSWORTH.

J. H. TENNEY.

1 Lo, the zeph - yr, soft - ly breath-ing, Wakes the earth a - gain;
2 Lo, the show - ers, gen - tly fall - ing, Buds and flow - ers bring;
3 Lo, the sun - light, soft - ly beam-ing, Gives a hun - dred fold;

But the spir - it soft - ly plead - ing, Stirs the hearts of men.
Through the gen - tle spir - its call - ing, Hearts are made to sing.
But the grac - es of the spir - it, Yield the fruit un - told.

CHORUS.

Pre - cious spir - it! pre-cious spir - it! Breath on us to - day:
Precious spir-it! Precious spir-it! Breath on us to - day:

Ten - der spir - it! ten - der spir - it! Leave us not we pray.
Ten-der spir-it! ten-der spir-it! Leave us not we pray.

11

THE HEAVENLY GLORY.

A. S KIEFFER.

1 Far from these nar - row scenes of night Un-bound - ed glo - ries rise,
2 Fair, dis - tant, land could mor - tal eyes But half thy charms ex - plore,
3 No clouds those bliss - ful re - gions know, Realms ev - er bright and fair;
4 Pre - pare us, Lord, by grace di - vine, For thy bright courts on high:

And realms of joy and pure de-light Un-known to mor-tal eyes.
How would our spir - its long to fly And dwell on earth no more.
For sin, the source of mor - tal woe, Can nev - er en - ter there.
Then bid our spir - its rise and join The chor - us of the sky.

bright glo - ry land,

CHORUS.

In that bright glo - ry land, In that bright glo - ry land, Shall we

When the toil

dwell in that land ev - er - more, ev - er - more; When the toil and the strife,

12

THE HEAVENLY GLORY.

and the strife *ritard.*

When the toil and the strife Of this wea - ry, wea-ry life are o'er.

I WOULD NOT LIVE ALWAY.

Slowly.

Arr. from HANDEL, by J. H. T.

1 I would not live al - way: I ask not to stay, Where
2 I would not live al - way: no, wel - come the tomb! Since
3 Oh, who would live al - way, a - way from his God, A-
4 Where the saints of all a - ges in harmony meet, Their

storm af - ter storm ris - es dark o'er the way; The few luc - id mornings that
Je - sus hath lain there, I dread not its gloom; There sweet be my rest, till he
way from yon heav - en, that bliss-ful a - bode, Where the riv-ers of pleas-ure flow
Sa - viour and breth-ren trans-port-ed to greet: While the anthems of rap - ture un-

dawn on us here Are e-nough for life's woes, full e - nough for its cheer.
bid me a - rise To hail him in tri - umph, de - scend-ing the skies.
o'er the bright plains, And the noontide of glo - ry e - ter - nal - ly reigns.
ceas-ing - ly roll, And the smile of the Lord is the feast of the soul.

13

I LONG TO GO HOME.

Mrs. E. W. CHAPMAN.

1 I long to go home to the land of rest, To the man - sions bright and fair, Oh, when shall I see the dear Sa - viour's face, And be - hold his glo - ry there!

2 I long to go home, and my spir - it yearns, For the dear ones gone be - fore; Oh, when shall I cross o'er the si - lent sea, To the loved on E - den's shore.

3 Oh, when shall I pass thro' the gold - en gate, And the crys - tal sea be - hold; Oh, when shall I eat of the ree of life, And a - bide in Je - sus' fold.

CHORUS.

I long to go home, yes, long to go home, Where sin shall not grieve me

14

I LONG TO GO HOME.

more; I long for the rest in the land of the blest,—Sweet

rest on that beau-ti - ful shore, Sweet rest on that beau-ti - ful shore.

SHINING DEW DROPS.

1 See the shi - ning dew - drops, On the flow - ers strew'd ;
2 See the morn - ing sun - beams, Light - ing up the wood ;
3 Hear the mount - ain stream - let, In the sol - i - tude;

Prov - ing as they spark - le, God is ev - er good.
Si - lent - ly pro - claim - ing, God is ev - er good.
With its rip - ples say - ing, God is ev - er good.

Rev. E. A. HOFFMAN. # THE LITTLE PILGRIM. A. S. KIEFFER.

1 The world looks ve - ry pret - ty, And beau - ti - ful to me;
2 I'm but a lit - tle pil - grim, My jour-ney's just be - gun;
3 Then like a lit - tle pil - grim, What-ev - er I may meet,

The sun shines out in glo - ry, On ev' - ry thing I see.
They say I shall meet sor - row, Be - fore my jour - ney's done.
I'll take it— joy or sor - row, And lay at Je - sus' feet.

I know I shall be hap - py, While in the world I stay,
The world is full of sor - row And suf - fer - ing they say;
He'll com - fort me in trou - ble, He'll wipe my tears a - way;

For I will fol - low Je - sus all the way.
But I will fol - low Je - sus all the way.
With joy I'll fol - low Je - sus all the way.

16

HEAVENLY REST.

A. S. KIEFFER. Arr. by J. H. TENNEY.

Andante.

1 I long for that sweet rest That comes when life is o'er, In
2 Oh, sweet - ly fair and pure That land to me ap - pears; A
3 A few more years of pain, And earth - ly toil, and strife, And

yon - der man - sions of the blest Be - yond death's sa - ble shore.
bliss - ful realm that lies se - cure, From dark - ness, death, and tears.
Christ's dear chil - dren all will gain, That home of bliss - ful life.

There my Re-deem - er lives, and rules, and reigns a - bove. And
Each day that pass - es by, but wafts us near - er there; And
Then let us sweet - ly live in love, and praise, and pray'r, And

rit.   *pp*

to his cho- sen chil-dren gives, a life of end - less love.
joy, and rests a - waits on high, in Zi - on bright and fair.
each at last from Christ re - ceive, a crown of glo - ry there.

17

W. A. OGDEN. **I LONG TO BE THERE.*** A. G. ABBEY.

1 I've a home far a-way, in the re-gions im-mor-tal, And
2 In that home far a-way, flows a beau-ti-ful riv-er, A
3 I have kin-dred and friends round that throne by the riv-er, Which
4 I am jour-ney-ing on to my home by the riv-er, And

Je-sus my Sa-viour is there; And sin can-not en-ter that
throne and a king-dom are there; They've built on its mar-gin and
stands in that coun-try so fair; They wait for me now and they
soon all its glo-ries I'll share! I'll dwell with my Sa-viour and

heav-en-ly por-tal, }
heav-en-ly por-tal, } I long, oh, I long to be there.
beck-on me o-ver, }
lov'd ones for-ev-er. }

CHORUS.

There the flow'rs ev-er spring, And the sweet warblers sing, 'Mid the

From "ALWAYS WELCOME," by per.
18

I LONG TO BE THERE.

groves in the coun-try so fair; There the bright an - gels stand, Ev - er-

more in that land, I long, oh, I long to be there.

A. S. K.

MY TREASURE.

A. S. KIEFFER.

1 I love the bless - ed Sa - viour, Who guards me day by day;
2 His arm is round a - bout me, Where-ev - er I may go;
3 His love I can - not mea - sure, So full, so pure, so free;

I'll seek his gra - cious fav - or To bless me all the way.
And he a - lone can keep me From sor - row, sin, and woe.
My Sa - viour is my treas - ure, And he will walk with me.

SHALL WE ALL BE THERE?

C. H. GABRIEL.

A. J. SHOWALTER.

1 Shall we all ar-rive in glo-ry, At the set-ting of life's sun?
2 Shall we cross the storm-y bil-lows, And yon peace-ful har-bor gain?
3 Shall we hear the heav'n-ly mu-sic, That the saints a - lone can make?
4 Yes, oh, yes, my wea-ry bro-ther, All these things we soon shall know;

Shall we join the songs of an-gels, When the cares of life are done?
Shall we wear the robes of whiteness, Nev-er more to know a pain?
Shall we join those glad im-mor-tals, When in Je-sus we a-wake?
There in heav'n we'll reign for-ev-er, Free from sor-row, pain and woe.

Shall we know the bless-ed Sa-viour, When we see him o-ver there?
Shall we, in that gold-en ci-ty, Walk with Christ our Saviour there?
Shall we meet and know the lov'd ones, That have gone be-fore us there?
There, while rolls e-ter-nal a-ges, Shi-ning bright as noonday sun;

rit.

Shall we wear the crown for-ev-er, And the bliss of an-gels share?
Shall we lean on him for-ev-er, Nev-er-more to know a care?
Shall we clasp their hands in glo-ry, With our Sa-viour bright and fair?
We shall shout and sing in gladness, Nev-er shall our song be done.

FRANCES R. HAVERGAL. **WHOSE I AM.** A. J. SHOWALTER.

1 Je - sus, Mas - ter, whose I am, Purchased thine a - lone to be
2 Oth - er lords have long held sway; Now, thy name a - lone to bear;
3 Je - sus, Mas - ter, I am thine! Keep me faith - ful, keep me near:

By thy blood, O spot - less Lamb! Shed so wil - ling - ly for me:
Thy dear voice a - lone o - bey, Is my dai - ly, hour - ly pray'r.
Let thy pres - ence in me shine, All my home - ward way to cheer.

Let my heart be all thine own, Let me live to thee a - lone;
Whom have I in heav'n but thee? Noth - ing else my joy can be;
Je - sus! at thy feet I fall; Oh, be thou my all in all;

Let my heart be all thine own, Let me live to thee a - lone.
Whom have I in heav'n but thee? Noth - ing else my joy can be.
Je - sus! at thy feet I fall; Oh, be thou my all in all.

21

BERTHA.

IN THY HANDS.

W. P. CHAMBERS.

1 In thy hands, dear Lord, where else could I be,
2 In thy hands, dear Lord, to chis - el and mould,
3 In thy hands, dear Lord, I re - joice to be there,

So safe as with him who car - eth for me,
As seem - eth thee good, to strike or with - hold,
I yield all I have to thy cov - e - nant care,

Whose wis - dom and love, are great as his pow'r,
Un - til thou hast formed, of the hard stub - born clay,
To live or to die, chose thou as is best,

To cheer and sus - tain in each per - il - ous hour.
A ves - sel for use in thy own cho - sen way.
But fit me in love for my heav - en - ly rest.

22

ALL IS WELL.

J. H. T.

1 Through the love of God our Sa - viour, All will be well;
2 Though we pass through trib - u - la - tion, All will be well;
3 We ex - pect a bright to - mor - row; All will be well;

Free and change - less is his fa - vor; All, all is well;
Ours is such a full sal - va - tion, All, all is well;
Faith can sing through days of sor - row, All, all is well;

Pre - cious is the blood that healed us; Per - fect is the grace that sealed us;
Hap - py, still in God con - fid - ing, Fruit - ful, if in Christ a - bid - ing,
On our Fa - ther's love re - ly - ing, Je - sus ev' - ry need sup - ply - ing,

Strong the hand stretched ont to shield us; All must be well.
Ho - ly, through the spir - it guid - ing, All must be well.
Or in liv - ing, or in dy - ing, All must be well.

23

THERE'S LIGHT OVER THERE.*

Mrs. E. W. CHAPMAN.   J. H. TENNEY.

1 When the way seems long and drea - ry, And thy
2 When the hours seem dark and lone - ly, Fill'd with
3 Ev - er in his love a - bid - ing, Strong in

limbs are weak and wea - ry, Still pur - sue the path of
grief and sor - row on - ly, Then the watch - word keep in
faith and hope con - fid - ing, Keep in view the man - sions

right: "At eve - ning time it shall be light."
sight: "At eve - ning time it shall be light."
bright: "At eve - ning time it shall be light."

CHORUS.

There's light   o - ver there,   o - ver there, There's light o-ver
     O - ver there,   o - ver there,   There's

* From "SPIRITUAL SONGS," by per.

THERE'S LIGHT OVER THERE.

there,
The bliss of that beau - ti - ful place

light o - ver there,
The bliss of that beau-

Will all thoughts of thy sor - row ef - face.
There's

ti - ful place,
Will all thoughts of thy sor - row ef-

light o - ver there, o - ver there,
There's

face,
There's light o - ver there,

o - ver there.

light o - ver there, There's light o - ver there.

o - ver there,

o - ver there, o - ver there.

TAKE THE PRAISE WE BRING THEE.

J. H. ROSECRANS.

1 Take the praise we bring thee, Lord,   Something more than what we speak,
2 Look-ing back the way we've come,   What a sight, O Lord, we see!
3 We will shun no fu - ture storm,   Sure thy voice is in its wind;

For the love with - in us feels,   Words un - cer-tain, cold and weak.
All the fail - ure in our - selves;   All the love and strength in thee.
We'll con - front each com - ing cloud,   Sure the sun is bright be - hind.

Thoughts that rise and tears that fall, Praise thee bet - ter,—take them all.
Yet it seems so dark be - fore, Would that we had trust - ed more!
Pray - ing then, or prais - ing now, On - ly wilt thou teach us how.

NEVER ALONE.

J. McP.   JOHN McPHERSON.

1 Far out on the deep roll - ing o - cean, The sail - or rides o - ver the
2 And deep in the earth works the min - er; Death lurks in the walls all a-
3 Lord, guide till we cross the dark riv - er, Whose wa-ters are flow - ing be-

NEVER ALONE.

sea,   A - lone 'mid this migh - ty com - mo - tion,   Where
round,   He trusts in an eye that is high - er,   Whose
tween   This life and thy own bright for - ev - er,   Where

CHORUS.

num - ber - less dan - gers be.
care ev - er will a - bound.   }   Yet, nev - er a - lone is the
all is so calm, se - rene!

Chris - tian Whose trust is in faith and prayer,

For God is a Friend un-fail - ing, And he is ev' - ry - where.

27

I HAVE FOUND JESUS.

E. R. LATTA.

*

1 I have found Je - sus, Of whom the prophets spake; I have found Je - sus, Who
2 I have found Je - sus, So gen-tle, meek and mild; I have found Je - sus, And
3 I have found Je - sus, And he shall be my Guide; I have found Je - sus, And

suf - fered for my sake; When I be-sought him, He lis-tened to my plea;
I am now his child: Come to the Sa - viour, My spir - it heard him say;
in his wounds I hide; Him let me fol - low, And nev - er him de - ny;

CHORUS.

He is the fair - est, Of all the fair to me!
And when I found him, He turned me not a - way! } I have found Je - sus!
Take me, dear Sa - viour, To glo - ry when I die!

I have found Je - sus! Dear bless - ed Je - sus; Who suf - fered for me!

A. S. K.

AFTER WHILE.

A. S. KIEFFER.

1 { Earth - ly cares will soon be end - ed, Af - ter
   { Hearts and hands with dust be blend - ed, Af - ter

D. C. Shall find rest where skies are chee - ry, Af - ter

FINE.

while, af - ter while; } And our feet, now worn and
while, af - ter while; }

while, af - ter while.

D. C.

wea - ry With life's path - way, dark and drea - ry,

2

We shall hail a happy morning
After while, after while.
Zion's hills with light adorning,
After while, after while;
Even now sweet spirits meet us,
And to come to them entreat us,
At heaven's portals they will greet us
After while, after while.

3

There beside the crystal river,
After while, after while,
We shall praise thee, glorious Giver,
After while, after while.
And through all the glad forever,
We shall live with Jesus ever,
And shall part, no, never, never,
After while, after while.

29

HOME ON THE EVERGREEN SHORE.

NEVA E. PARKHILL.

R. A. KINZIE.

1 Ov - er the riv - er I hear the song
2 Ov - er the riv - er I hear the song
3 Ov - er the riv - er I hear the song

Ech - o - ing o'er and o'er, Life will ye find in the
Ech - o - ing o'er and o'er, Love will ye find near the
Ech - o - ing o'er and o'er, Peace will ye find, O ye

glo - ri - fied one, At home on the ev - er - green shore.
heav - en - ly throne, Where sor - row shall grieve thee no more.
wan - der - ers come, And rest on the ev - er - green shore.

Oh, the ev - er - green shore, Where the an - gels dwell, Where

HOME ON THE EVERGREEN SHORE.

loud the ech - o - ing an - thems swell! Pure and sweet are the

tales they tell Of home, on the ev - er - green shore.

JEWEL. 7s.

F. L. ARMSTRONG.

1 Christ, of all my hopes the ground, Christ, the spring of all my joy!
2 Fount-ain of o'er - flow-ing grace! Free - ly from thy full-ness give;
3 Firm - ly trust-ing in thy blood, Noth - ing shall my breast con - found;
4 Thus, oh, thus an en-trance give To the land of cloud-less sky;

Still in thee let me be found; Still for thee my pray'rs em - ploy.
Till I close my earth - ly race, Be it "Christ for me to live."
Safe -ly I shall pass the flood, Safe -ly reach Im - man-uel's ground.
Hav-ing known it "Christ to live," Let me know it "gain to die."

31

BLESSED NAME, HOW SWEET!

A. S. KIEFFER.

1 How sweet the name of Je - sus sounds In a be - liev - er's ear,
2 Weak is the ef - fort of our hearts, And cold our warm-est thoughts,
3 Till then we would thy love pro-claim With ev' - ry fleet - ing breath,

It soothes his sor - rows, heals his wounds, And drives a - way his fear.
But when we see thee as thou art, We'll praise thee as we ought.
And may the mu - sic of thy name Re - fresh our souls in death.

REFRAIN.

Bless - ed name, how sweet, Bless - ed
name, bless - ed name, how sweet it sounds,

name, Oh, how sweet! Bless - ed name, how
Bless - ed name, oh, how sweet it sounds, name, how sweet . .

BLESSED NAME, HOW SWEET!

sweet, How sweet the name of Je - sus sounds.
it sounds,

CORONATION. C. M.

OLIVER HOLDEN.

1 All hail the power of Je-sus' name! Let an-gels pros-trate fall:
2 Crown him, ye mar-tyrs of our God, Who from his al-tar call;
3 Ye cho-sen seed of Is-rael's race, A rem-nant weak and small,
4 Ye Gen-tile sin-ners, ne'er for-get The wormwood and the gall;

Bring forth the roy - al di - a - dem, And crown him Lord of all!
Ex - tol the stem of Jes-se's rod, And crown him Lord of all!
Hail him who saves you by his grace, And crown him Lord of all!
Go, spread your tro-phies at his feet, And crown him Lord of all!

Bring forth the roy-al di - a - dem, And crown him Lord of all!
Ex - tol the stem of Jes - se's rod, And crown him Lord of all!
Hail him who saves you by his grace, And crown him Lord of all!
Go, spread your trophies at his feet, And crown him Lord of all!

WE ARE SINGING.*

CHAS. H. GABRIEL.   P. P. BLISS.

1 We are sing-ing, prais-es bring-ing, To our Sa-viour to-day,
2 He hath led us, kind-ly fed us With sweet man-na di-vine;
3 Care and tri-als, self de-ni-als Meet we day af-ter day;
4 Broth-er, love him, come and prove him Your Re-deem-er and King;

For his kind-ness, in our blind-ness, Lead-ing safe-ly al-way.
Gen-tly chid-ing, ere a-bid-ing On our path-way to shine.
But so sweet-ly and com-plete-ly Je-sus drives them a-way.
He'll re-ceive you and re-lieve you: Hal-le-lu-jah then sing.

CHORUS.

Hal-le-lu-jah! hal-le-lu-jah! Roll the mu-sic a-long:

Christ and glo-ry, wondrous sto-ry, Is the theme of our song.

* From D. C. Cook's S. S. Teacher's and Scholar's Quarterly.

JESUS, LOVER OF MY SOUL.

G. R. STREET.

1 Je - sus, Lov-er of my soul, Let me to thy bos-om fly,
2 Oth - er re-fuge have I none: Hangs my help-less soul on thee:
3 All my trust on thee is stayed; All my help from thee I bring;

While the billows near me roll, While the tem-pest still is high.
Leave, ah, leave me not a - lone; Still sup-port and com-fort me.
Cov - er my de-fenceless head With the shad-ow of thy wing

REFRAIN.

Hide me, O my Sa-viour, hide me Till the storm of life be past;

Safe in - to the ha-ven guide me: Oh, re-ceive my soul at last!

35

WORK AND PRAY.

PRISCILLA J. OWENS.   J. H. TENNEY.

1 This our con-stant mot-to be, Work and pray, work and pray:
2 We a Sa-viour's love re-peat, Work and pray, work and pray;
3 Grow-ing strong-er by and by, Work and pray, work and pray;
4 Youth-ful lips may plead in pray'r, Work and pray, work and pray;

We can hear the heathen's plea, Moan-ing sad-der than the sea;
Had we an-gel's pin-ion's fleet, Swift-er bear the ti-dings sweet,
We can lift a torch on high, That will show a Sa-viour nigh,
Youth-ful hearts Christ's love may share, Youth-ful hearts his cross may bear,

Give with rea-dy hands and free, Work and pray, work and pray.
Yet we move with will-ing feet, Work and pray, work and pray.
Kin-dle all their darkened sky, Work and pray, work and pray.
Youth-ful brows his crown shall wear, Work and pray, work and pray.

CHORUS.

Al-ways work and pray, Al-ways work and pray,
Always work, yes, work and pray, Always work, yes, work and pray,

36

WORK AND PRAY.

Give with rea - dy hands and free,
Yet we move with wil - ling feet,
Kin - dle all their dark-ened sky,
Youth - ful brows his crown shall wear,

Al - ways work and pray.
Al - ways work and pray.

HOME OF THE BLEST.

ALDINE.   A. S. KIEFFER.

1 Home of the blest, sweet vis - ions of love Glad-den my
2 Harps of the blest, your mu - sic I hear: Sooth-ing - ly
3 Home of the blest, life's bur - dens I'll bear: Walk-ing by

soul while think-ing of thee Sweet are thy streams and gardens a-
sweet it comes un - to me, Calm-ing to rest each tor-tur - ing
faith thy glo-ries I see; Short - ly thy joys and pleasures I'll

bove ; —
fear ;   Home of the blest, thou art dear - er than all to me.
share ;

37

E. R. LATTA. # I AM STILL WITH THEE. J. H. TENNEY.

1 I am still with Thee, Wher-e'er I stray; I am still with
2 I am still with Thee, In bliss or woe; I am still with
3 I am still with Thee, Though far I rove; I am still with
4 I am still with Thee, Though from my sight Thou art hid - den

Thee, By night and day: On the morn-ing's wings Though I re - pair,
Thee, I joy - ous know On Thy arm of might My soul shall lean,
Thee, And feel thy love; In each try - ing hour Be Thou my Friend,
still By day and night; When the vale of death My feet shall near,

CHORUS.

To the farthest bound, The Lord is there!
When the storm is loud, Or sky ser - ene!
And my journey through My steps at - tend.
May thy presence quell My ev' - ry fear.
In that home a - bove, . . Oh,
In that home, that home above, Oh,

let me be, For - ev - er - more, Dear Lord, with thee.
let me, dear Fa-ther be, For - ev - er, for - ev - er-more,

38

INVITATION.

1 Come, ye wan-d'rers, now for-sa-ken, Come, and let your souls find rest;
2 Saints are wait-ing, an-gels long-ing, God, in-vit-ing, "chil-dren come;"
3 Christ is will-ing to for-give you; On-ly seek and you shall find;
4 Come, then, wea-ry, hea-vy la-den, Throw your bur-dens all a-side;

Come, and join the heav'nly chor-us; Come, and jour-ney with the blest.
Why now lin-ger? why not heed them? Why not seek e-ter-nal rest?
He it was that suf-fered for you; He has died for all man-kind.
Come and claim the bless-ed Je-sus; 'Tis for you the Lord hath died.

CHORUS.

Come, ye wea-ry, hea-vy la-den; Come, and let your souls be blest,

Come to Christ, the liv-ing fountain; "Come, and I will give you rest."

39

THE EVERGREEN SHORE.

A. S. KIEFFER.

Gently.

1 Be - yond the dark val - ley and shad - ow and death, There
2 Bright man - sions of splen - dor a - dorn that fair shore, Still
3 'Tis there that our Sa - viour a place has pre - pared,— A
4 Oh, why should we wan - der, in fol - ly and sin, A -

bloom- eth an ev - er-green shore ; Se - cure from all chan-ges of
wa - ters of life mur-mur there; The glo - ry of God and the
rest for the sheep of his fold; With A - bram and I - saac and
way from that ev - er-green shore ; When Christ in his mer - cy our

sea - son or time, Where tem - pests and clouds are no more.
smiles of his love, A - dorn it with ra - di - ance rare.
Ja - cob to share The joys that can nev - er be told.
souls doth en - treat To share its pure joys ev - er - more?

CHORUS.

There's rest on that beau - ti - ful shore, Sweet
shore, bright shore,

40

THE EVERGREEN SHORE.

rest on that ev - er - green shore, Where sor-row and sigh - ing and
shore, sweet rest,

dark-ness and death And tem - pests and clouds are no more.

GOING HOME.

POPULAR MELODY.

1 { My heav'nly home is bright and fair; Nor pain nor death can en - ter there: }
{ Its glit-t'ring tow'rs the sun out-shine; That heav'nly man-sion shall be mine. }

CHORUS.

{ I'm go - ing home, I'm go - ing home, I'm go - ing home to die no more. }
{ To die no more, To die no more, I'm go - ing home to die no more. }

2
My Father's house is built on high,
Far, far above the starry sky;
When from this earthly prison free,
That heavenly mansion mine shall be.

3
Let others seek a home below,
Which flames devour, or waves o'erflow;
Be mine a happier lot to own
A heavenly mansion near the throne.

41

COME UNTO HIM.

P. P. BLISS.

Tenderly.

1 Come un - to me when shad - ows dark - ly gath - er,
2 Ye who have mourned when flow'r - ets sweet were ta - ken,
3 Large are the man - sions in thy Fa - ther's dwell - ing,

When the sad heart is wea - ry and dis - tressed,
When the ripe fruit fell rich - ly to the ground,
And the glad homes that sor - rows nev - er dim;

Seek - ing for com - fort from your heav'n - ly Fa - ther,
When loved ones slept in bright - er homes to wa - ken,
Sweet are the harps in ho - ly mu - sic swell - ing;

Come un - to me, and I will give you rest.
Where now their brows with spir - it wreaths are crowned.
Soft are the tones which raise the heav'n - ly hymn.

THE TWILIGHT FALLS.

Andante.

1 The twi-light falls, the night is near, I fold my work a - way,
2 The old, old sto - ry,— yet I kneel To tell it at thy call,
3 So here I lay me down to rest, As night - ly shad-ows fall,

And kneel to One who bends to hear The sto - ry of the day.
And cares grow light - er as I feel That Je - sus knows them all.
And lean con -fid - ing on His breast Who knows and pit - ies all.

REFRAIN.

The sto - ry of the day, The sto - ry of the day;
That Je - sus knows them all, That Je - sus knows them all;
Who knows and pit - ies all, Who knows and pit - ies all;

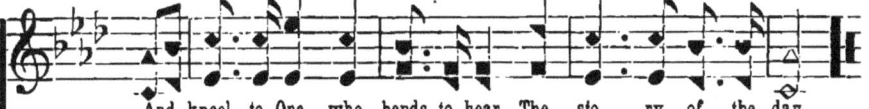

And kneel to One who bends to hear The sto - ry of the day.
And cares grow light - er as I feel That Je - sus knows them all.
And lean con - fid - ing on His breast Who knows and pit - ies all.

SABBATH-SCHOOL WELCOME.

Mrs. E. C. ELLSWORTH.

O. W. BENTLEY.

1 Wel - come, friends, we give you greet-ing; Wel-come to the Sabbath-school!
2 Fath - ers, moth - ers, bring your chil - dren; Suf - fer lit - tle ones to come;
3 Here we learn of gen - tle Je - sus; Sit with Ma - ry at his feet;

Has - ten! 'tis the hour of meet-ing: Come, and let the place be full.
Teach - ers, go in - to the by - ways, Lead the lit - tle wan -d'rers home.
Learn to know and do his pleas - ure; Thus for heav - en we are meet.

CHORUS.

Wel-come, wel-come, wel - come, Dear - est friends, we bid you wel - come;
Welcome, welcome,

Wel-come, wel-come, wel - come, Wel-come to the Sab-bath - school.
Wel-come, welcome,

44

WALK BY FAITH A LITTLE LONGER.

T. F. W.

1 What tho' clouds are round a - bout thee, Earth seems dark, and cold, and
2 There no cloud shall dim the vis - ion: All is light and warmth and
3 What tho' none are left to love thee, No one thou canst call thine

drear; Sure -ly there's a bet - ter coun-try Than we've ev - er dreamed of here.
love; There's a home for all the homeless In "our Fath-er's house" a - bove.
own; He has said, "I'm with thee alway;" Fear not: thou art not a - lone.

CHORUS.

Walk by faith a lit - tle long - er: Keep thy heart all free from

guile; Soon thou'lt hear the bless-ed Mas-ter Say, "Well done! come home, my child."

45

OH, TO CHEER US.

Mrs. E. C. ELLSWORTH.

J. H. TENNEY.

1 Oh, to cheer us, be thou near us, Dear-est Sa-viour, Friend di - vine!
2 Fee - bly groping, dim-ly hop - ing, Oft we fal - ter in our way,
3 Hearts are turning, and are burn - ing With de - sire to know the Lord,

Oft our blindness hides thy kind - ness, And in dark-ness we re - pine.
Up-ward glancing, faith ad - vanc - ing, Sees the dawn of com - ing day.
Yet in un - ion, earth's com-mun - ion, Love must trust the Saviour's word.

CHORUS.

But in glo - ry, love's sweet sto - ry Wakes the soul to life a - new;

And in brightness, ra-diant bright - ness, Face to face our Lord we view.

46

ROOM AT THE CROSS.

W. B. B.   WM. B. BLAKE.

Duet.

1 Room at the Cross for a trembling soul, Room at the Cross for you;
2 Room at the Cross for a breaking heart, Room at the Cross for you;
2 Room at the Cross for earth's weary and worn, Room at the Cross for you;

Where the sin - la - den may be made whole, Room at the Cross for you.
Choose, then, like Ma - ry, the bet - ter part, Room at the Cross for you.
Come, then, oh, come, then, ye souls who mourn, Room at the Cross for you.

REFRAIN.

Room, room, room at the Cross, Room at the Cross for you,

Room, room, room at the Cross, Room at the Cross for you.

LEAD ME.

J. H. TENNEY.

1 Lead me, O my Shep-herd, lead me, Where the up-per pas-tures grow,
2 Lead me, O my Shep-herd, lead me, Up-ward from the mis-ty plain,
3 Till I stand where from thy pres-ence, Earthward all the shad-ows roll,

Where from rocks thy rod hath riv-en, Clear-er, cool-er foun-tains flow.
Till be-neath me lie the val-leys, Till the sun-lit heights I gain.
Up-ward to those heav'n-ly pas-tures, Lead me, Shep-herd of my soul.

CHORUS.

Where thou lead-est I will fol-low, Though the way be

steep and drear; Bright will seem the dark-est path-way,

48

LEAD ME.

While the Shep-herd's voice I hear, While the Shepherd's voice I hear.

LISTEN! HE IS THERE.

Rev. J. E. RANKIN, D. D.

J. H. TENNEY.

1 Lis-ten! lis-ten! he is there, Knocking, knocking, worn with care:
2 Lis-ten! lis-ten! thee he seeks; Knocking, knocking, yes, he speaks:
3 Lis-ten! lis-ten! at the door, Knocking, knocking, o'er and o'er:
4 Lis-ten! lis-ten! still the same: Knocking, knocking, 'twas thy name:

'Tis the King-ly One, the Stran - ger, He who came from glo - ry down:
What! poor soul, dost thou not know him? With nightdews his locks are wet:
"Sin - ner, sin - ner, long I've sought thee!" This he says to you and me:
Hark his ac - cents, soft and ten - der! Yes, I will un - bar the door:

Cra-dled once in Bethlehem's man - ger, Wearing now of thorns a crown.
Sure-ly, thou wilt kindness show him; What thou ow'st,dost thou for - gets.
"On the cross,with blood I've bought thee: Wilt thou not my foll'wer be?"
En - ter! I make full sur - ren - der: Reign with-in me, ev - er - more.

4

49

BEYOND THE JORDAN'S FLOOD.

M. F. S.

H. F. STIPES,

1 There's a land be-yond this drea-ry world, I know, There's a
2 Sin and sor - row ev-er-more will be unknown, To the
3 Soon we'll rest be-yond the tur-bid Jor - dan's strand, Soon for

hap - py home for you and me, Smil-ing bright and fair beyond earth's
saints who dwell up-on that shore; Je - sus there will reign up-on his
us the gates will o - pen wide; There for - ev - er we shall rest at

drea - ry shore; All its glo - rious splen-dors sure we'll see.
gold - en throne, And with him we'll wor - ship ev - er - more.
God's right hand, Far be - yond Death's dark and drea - ry tide.

REFRAIN.

A home of peace for you and me; Sweet

50

BEYOND THE JORDAN'S FLOOD.

home be - yond life's drea - ry shore; Its shi - ning por - tals by and

by we'll see, And will dwell with Je - sus ev - er - more.

GENTLENESS. S. M.

E. HAMILTON.

Slowly.

1 My Fa - ther's house on high, Is my e - ter - nal home;
2 My Fa - ther and my God, Oh, lead me safe - ly on,
3 Then join the heav'n - ly throng To sing re - deem - ing love;

O God, for - bid that I should sigh, While trav'ling here a - lone.
Till in that heav'nly world a - bove I feel my work is done.
While end - less a - ges roll a - long, We'll praise our God a - bove.

THERE'LL BE LIGHT BY AND BY.

Mrs. E. W. CHAPMAN.

J. H. TENNEY.

1 The mist - y clouds hang round my way, So
2 I find as through life's thorn - y path I
3 Oh, keep me in the nar - row way; En-

dark I can - not see; But hope es - pies a
walk with wea - ry feet, Each cloud a sil - ver
close my hand in thine, Nor let me from thee

bright - er ray, And says, "God lead - eth thee."
lin - ing hath; God makes the bit - ter sweet.
ev - er stray, Thou blest Re - deem - er, mine!

CHORUS.

There'll be light by and by, There'll be light by and by, There'll be

THERE'LL BE LIGHT BY AND BY.

light by and by, by and by; No

There'll be light by and by,

shad - ows can fall on the glit - ter - ing strand; No

dark - ness pre - vail in that beau - ti - ful land: There'll be

rit. e dim.

light by and by, by and by, by and by.

FAR O'ER THE SEA.

1 There's a beau - ti - ful ha - ven far o - ver the sea, Where
2 There are heav - en - ly man - sions far o - ver the sea, That
3 There's a rest for the wea - ry far o - ver the sea, And

loved ones have gone on be - fore; And there they are wait - ing and
shine with the light of God's face, And there is a man - sion in
pil - grims may claim it as theirs; For I know there's a rest in

watch - ing for me, To land on that beau - ti - ful shore;
wait - ing for me, A - way in that beau - ti - ful place.
wait - ing for me, That comes af - ter sad - ness and cares.

The riv - er is shad - owed by sor - row and woe, 'Tis
A white robe I'll wear in that heav - en - ly home, Though
In that beau - ti - ful ci - ty far o - ver the sea, We shall

FAR O'ER THE SEA.

dark as the hour ere the dawn; But I shall land safe - ly and
wick - ed and sin - ful I am; I know that my Sa - viour has
dwell when life's jour - ney is o'er From pain and from sor - row, from

sure - ly I know, If on - ly my Guide leads me on.
bid - den me "come," And wash in the blood of the Lamb.
wea - ri - ness free, Where Je - sus a - waits on the shore.

SOLITUDE.

A. J. SHOWALTER.

1 I love to steal a - while a - way, From ev' - ry cum - b'ring care,
2 I love to think of mer - cies past, And fu - ture good im - plore;
3 I love by faith to take a view, Of bright-er scenes in heav'n,

And spend the hours of set - ting day In hum-ble, grate - ful pray'r.
And all my cares and sor - rows cast On Him whom I a - dore.
The pros - pect doth my strength re- new, While here by tem - pests driven.

NO NIGHT IN HEAVEN.

Rev. E. W. LAWHON. J. H. TENNEY.

1 No night in heav'n, that bless - ed clime, No gloom which marks these
2 No cloud to in - ter - cept the mind; No thought by nar - row
3 No night of sor - row there, we know; The heart shall ne'er be

years of time; The dwell - ers need no sun for light, The
bounds con-fined; In heav'n we shall more ful - ly know What
touched by woe; The Lord will wipe all tears a - way: Be -

CHORUS.

Lord him - self pre - cludes the night. ⎫
we have dim - ly seen be - low. ⎬ Oh, bless - ed thought, no
yond this night is heav - en's day, ⎭

night in heav'n, But one re - splen - dent, end - less day! We

NO NIGHT IN HEAVEN.

rest up-on the prom-ise given, And tread by faith the pil-grim way.

THE EDEN OF LOVE.

A. S. K.   A. S. KIEFFER.

1 Oh, when shall I dwell in my Fa-ther's bright home, From
2 Oh, fair are the halls in that pal-ace of song, And
3 There safe shall I rest when life's jour-ney is o'er, And

sor-row and sin ev-er free; With fair shin-ing an-gels for-
sweet-ly the ran-som'd ones sing, As a-ges of bliss flood their
sing with the loved ones a-bove; There dwell with my Sa-viour and

ev-er to roam, And my bless-ed Re-deem-er to see.
bright tide a-long In that home of the Sa-viour, our King.
friends ev-er-more In that sweet, hap-py E-den of love.

57

Rev. J. B. ATCHINSON.

HOLY BIBLE !*

F. L. ARMSTRONG.

1 Ho - ly Bi - ble! book di - vine, Light and life in ev' - ry line;
2 Ho - ly Bi - ble! book of truth! On - ly guide for age and youth;
3 Ho - ly Bi - ble! book of God! For man - kind the on - ly code;
4 Ho - ly Bi - ble! spir - its sword! Sto - ry of our bless - ed Lord;

Light for all who Christ re - ceive, Life for all who will be - lieve.
All who search are sure to find, Rest of soul and peace of mind.
All its laws we must o - bey, Heed its pre - cepts day by day.
Chart to guide me to the skies, Where a - waits the glo - ry - prize.

ff CHORUS.

Ho - ly Bi - ble! bless - ed book! Now by faith in thee I look;

O - pen thou my eyes, O Lord, To the won - ders of thy word.

From "EXALTED PRAISE," by per.

WHERE SHALL MY SOUL FIND REST?

Rev. E. A. HOFFMAN.   *

1 Oh, where shall my soul find a ha-ven of rest, Where anguish is
2 The home of the soul is in heav-en a-bove, The man-sions of
3 How sweet is the rest-ing with Je-sus in light, With-in the fair

hushed in each ach-ing breast? The earth has no home where the soul is at
pure and e-ter-nal love; Yes, there can the soul find a full-ness of
pa-la-ces gold-en bright, At home on the beau-ti-ful ev-er-green

CHORUS.

peace; There must be a land that is pur-er than this.
joy, Where sin and temp-ta-tion no more can an-noy.
shore, Where sor-row and sigh-ing for-ev-er are o'er.
} Oh, sweet, sweet

Repeat. pp

home! 'Neath thy gold-en dome, With Christ and the an-gels, I long to roam.

59

OH, SWEET HEAVEN!

Rev. E. A. HOFFMAN.

1 Soul, thy fet-tered wings un-fold, That I may my Lord be-hold
2 Mu-sic rolls o'er heav-en's plain; Oh, how sweet is the re-frain!
3 Oh, what pleas-ure there to dwell! Joy no hu-man tongue can tell!
4 Pa-ra-dise, se-rene and fair, How I long to waft me there!

My poor heart is full of long-ing; All my powers are up-ward
Had I pin-ions, had I pin-ions, I would leave these dark do-
Where the streets are pure and gold-en; Glo-rious all that is be-
'Neath the tree of life re-pos-ing, Heav'n its rich-est joys dis-

CHORUS.

thronging To the home of shin-ing gold.
min-ions, And would fly to E-den's plain.
hol-den In thy home, Im-man-u-el.
clos-ing; Sa-viour, give me entrance there.

Oh, sweet heav-en! home of

leas-ure! Oh, sweet heav-en! rich-est treas-ure. Soul, thy

OH, SWEET HEAVEN!

fet - tered wings un - fold! Mount to yon - der home of gold!

JESUS IS PRECIOUS.

Rev. W. F. COSNER.   G. B. STREET.

1 Je - sus is prec - ious; Je - sus is mine;
2 Je - sus is prec - ious: Far from the fold
3 Je - sus is prec - ious; Je - sus is strong;

Safe on his bos - om I would re-cline; From sin's de - file - ment,
Heed - less I wandered, Hung - ry and cold; Far o'er the mountains,
Bear - ing his weak ones Safe - ly a - long. To them who trust him,

Cleansed by his blood, By his free spir - it Brought back to God.
Rug - ged and bare, Sought he his lost one, Per - ish - ing there.
Strength shall be giv'n: Je - sus will lead them Safe home to heav'n.

OUR SABBATH HOME.

D. W. HINMAN.

J. H. TENNEY.

1 We meet a - gain, this Sab - bath day; Dear
2 Teach us the wis - dom of thy word; Show
3 Lead us where crys - tal riv - ers flow From

Lord, to thee we hum - bly pray: Fill
us the beau - ties of the Cross; For-
the pure foun - tain of thy love; Teach

all our hearts with Je - sus' love, And
bid that a - ny here, dear Lord, Should
us the har - mo - nies di - vine That

bless us from thy throne a - bove.
suf - fer an e - ter - nal loss.
ech - o round thy throne a - bove.

OUR SABBATH HOME.

CHORUS.

The Sun - day - school, ... our Sab - bath
The Sun - day-school,

home, . . With joy - ful hearts . . . and will - ing
our Sab - bath home, With joy - ful hearts

feet, . . We come, we come, . . We come to
and will - ing feet, We come, we come,

thee, . . For here our Sa - viour we shall meet.
we come to thee, For here our Sa - viour

63

W. T. D.

BY AND BY.*

Rev. W. T. DALE.

1 O - ver Jer - dan we shall meet, By and by; by and by;
2 All our sor - rows shall be past, By and by; by and by;
3 We shall join the heavenly choir, By and by; by and by;
4 There we'll join the ransomed throng, By and by; by and by;

In that hap - py land so sweet, By and by, by and by;
We shall reach our home at last, By and by, by and by;
We shall strike the gol - den lyre, By and by, by and by;
Chant - ing love's re - deem - ing song, By and by, by and by;

We shall gath - er on the shore With our kin - dred gone be - fore,
With the ran - somed we shall stand, There a ho - ly, hap - py band,
In our home so bright and fair, Where the hap - py an - gels are,
There we'll meet be - fore the throne, Then we'll lay our tro - phies down,

And the Sa - viour's name a - dore, By and by, by and by.
Crowned with glo - ry in that land, By and by, by and by.
We shall praise for - ev - er there, By and by, by and by.
And re - ceive a shin - ing crown, By and by, by and by.

*From "LAST WORDS," by per.

64

HE COMETH.*

GEO. C. HUGG.

1 Wide, ye heav'nly gates, un - fold,   Closed no more by death and sin;
2 He who God's pure law ful - filled;   Je - sus, the in - car - nate word;
3 "Who shall up to that a - bode   Fol - low in the Saviour's train?"
4 They whose dai - ly ac - tions prove   Stead - fast faith and ho - ly fear,

Lo! the conquering Lord be - hold;   Let the King of glo - ry in.
He whose truth with blood was sealed   He is heaven's all glo - rious Lord.
They who in his cleansing blood   Wash a - way each guil - ty stain.
Fer - vent zeal and grate - ful love;   They shall dwell for - ev - er here.

CHORUS.

Let him in; oh, let him in, Let the King of glo - ry in,

ritard.

Wel - come him, oh, wel-come him: Bles - sed Lord, come in, come in.

* From "EXALTED PRAISE," by per.

GOD IS WEIGHING YOU.

Rev. J. B. ATCHINSON.   A. S. KIEFFER.

"Thou art weighed in the balances and art found wanting."—DAN. v. 27.

1 God is weigh-ing you, my brother! And his bal-an-ces are true;
2 God is weigh-ing you, my brother! By the stand-ard of his word,
3 God is weigh-ing you, my brother! Weigh-ing ev'-ry se-cret thought,

Dare you tri-fle with him longer; Thoughtless, that he's weigh-ing you?
By your faith in his own promise, By your love for Christ, the Lord:
Weigh-ing ev'-ry word and action, Ev'-ry deed your life hath wrought:

Should he find you want-ing, brother, When the fi-nal test is given,
Does he find you want-ing, brother? Do you all his law o-bey?
Does he find you want-ing, brother? Oh, let ev'-ry thought be pure;

Sad, in-deed will be the sentence; *Banished ev-er-more from Heaven!*
Is your faith in him un-wav'ring? Do you serve him day by day?
Gen-tle words and lov-ing ac-tions: These, his fa-vor will se-cure.

66

REST IN HEAVEN.

Mrs. O. L. SHACKLOCK.

J. H. TENNEY.

1 Af - ter the toil and tur - moil, Af - ter the strife is past,
2 They who have fought and con - quered, Wag-ing a war with sin,
3 Rest for the worn and wea - ry, Shel - ter for all the lost,

Com - eth the peace God giv - eth,— Com - eth the rest at last.
In - to the heav'n - ly ci - ty Glad-ly will en - ter in.
And in the bless - ed ha - ven, An - chor the temp - est - toss'd.

CHORUS.

Rest, sweet rest for the wea - ry, Af - ter the toil and pain,

Rest, sweet rest for the wea - ry, Af - ter the toil, the toil and pain:

Sleep for the well be - lov - ed, Crowns will the vic - tors gain.

vic - tors gain.

Sleep for the well be - lov - ed, Crowns will the vic - tors gain.

67

WITH JESUS TO-DAY.

In a recitative manner.

1 I have been talk-ing with Je - sus to - day,
2 I have been walk-ing with Je - sus to - day,
3 I have been rest-ing with Je - sus to - day,

Humbly con - fess-ing my sin;
Walking so close by his side;
Leaning up - on his breast;

Trembling and knocking, I
Straying and help-less, I
Wea-ry with toil-ing, I

heard a voice say, "Child of my love, come in:"
heard a voice say, "Child, let me be your Guide:"
heard a voice say, "Come un - to me and rest:"

On - ly con - fes-sion to him I could make; On - ly sweet words of for-
Blessed as - sur-ance, my Sa-viour is near; Walk-ing with Je - sus, what
Leaning on Je - sus, my rest is com-plete; Bur - dens are lift - ed and

WITH JESUS TO-DAY.

give - ness he spake, Tell - ing me free - ly of grace to par - take;
have I to fear? E'en in the val - ley his pres - ence will cheer,
ser - vice is sweet; Rest - ing in Je - sus, oh, bliss - ful re - treat!

Stay with me, child : be clean.
Bear - ing me o'er the tide ;
Rest - ing with him I'm blest.

CHORUS.

Talk - ing with Je - sus, it
Walk - ing with Je - sus, I
Rest - ing with Je - sus, my

com - forts my heart ; Talk - ing with Je - sus sweet peace doth im - part ;
nev - er can stray ; Walk - ing with Je - sus, for he is the Way ;
soul's rest - ing - place, Rest - ing with Je - sus, re - freshed by his grace,

Talk-ing with Je - sus, no more will we part, Ev - er - more talk-ing with him.
Walk-ing with Je - sus in yon end-less day, Ev - er - more walk-ing with him.
Rest-ing with Je - sus a - bove, face to face, Ev - er - more rest- ing with him.

GOSPEL BANNER.

A. S. KIEFFER.

1 Now be the gos - pel ban - ner In ev' - ry land un - furl'd;
2 What though em - bat - tled le - gions Of earth and hell com - bine!
3 Yes! thou shalt reign for - ev - er, O Je - sus, King of kings!

And be the shout, Ho - san - na! Re - echo - ed through the world:
His arm throughout their re - gions Shall soon re - splen-dent shine;
Thy light, thy love, thy fa - vor, Each ran -somed cap - tive sings.—

Till ev' - ry isle and na - tion, Till ev' - ry tribe and tongue,
Ride on! O Lord, vic - to - ri - ous; Im - man - uel, Prince of peace:
The isles are for thee wait - ing; The des - erts learn thy praise:

Re - ceive the great sal - va - tion, And join the hap - py throng.
Thy tri - umph shall be glo - ri - ous; Thy em - pire still in - crease.
The hills and val -leys greet - ing, The long re - spon-ses raise.

70

I'LL WORK FOR JESUS.

E. P.

Mrs. EMMA PITT.

1 What have I ev-er done for Je-sus, Who did so much to res-cue me?
2 With cords of ten-der love, he drew me; While deep in wretched sin I lay.
3 From sins dark slumber he aroused me; Up-on the rocks he placed my feet;
4 Then let me ev-er work for Je-sus; This Friend so lov-ing and so true;

With his own arm brought my salvation, With his own blood he set me free!
Oh, for this boundless love and mer-cy, I'll speak his good-ness ev'-ry day.
His own new song of love he gave me: To him a-lone are praises meet.
Point sin-nors to their dear Re-deem-er; My home e-ter-nal keep in view.

CHORUS.

I'll work for Je-sus! I'll work for Je-sus! Work for Je-sus till I die.—

I'll work for Je-sus! I'll work for Je-sus! Then I'll dwell with him on high.

71

I LAY MY SINS ON JESUS.

DR. BONAR.   WM. B. BLAKE.

1 I lay my sins on Je - sus;— The spot - less Lamb of God;
2 I lay my wants on Je - sus; All full - ness dwells in him;

He takes them all and frees us From the ac - curs - ed load;
He heal - eth my dis - eas - es; He doth my soul re - deem:

I bring my guilt to Je - sus, To wash my crim - son stains
I lay my griefs on Je - sus, My bur - dens and my cares:

White in his blood most pre - cious, Till not a spot re - mains.
He from them all re - leas - es; He all my sor - row shares.

I LAY MY SINS ON JESUS.

White   in   his   blood,   Till not a spot re - mains.
From   them re - leas - es;   He all my sor - row shares.

In   his blood, his blood most pre-cious.
He from them, from them re - leas - es.

TOPLADY.

1

Rock of Ages, cleft for me,
Let me hide myself in thee;
Let the water and the blood,
From thy side, a healing flood,
Be of sin the double cure,—
Save me from wrath and make me pure.

2

Should my tears forever flow,
Should my zeal no languor know,
All for sin could not atone:
Thou must save, and thou alone.
In my hand no price I bring;
Simply to thy cross I cling.

3

While I draw this fleeting breath,
When mine eyelids close in death,
When I rise to worlds unknown,
See thee on thy judgment throne,—
Rock of Ages, cleft for me,
Let me hide myself in thee.

73

BEAUTIFUL MORNING.

FRANK M. DAVIS.

1 Beau-ti-ful morn - ing, wel-come thy dawn - ing! Speed not, ye mo -
2 Beau-ti-ful morn - ing, wel-come thy dawn - ing! Day when the Sa -
3 Beau-ti-ful morn - ing, wel-come thy dawn - ing! Type of the long

ments, so swift-ly a - way; Stay while I pon - der, think-ing with won - der
viour a - rose from the dead: Let the sun bright-en! let the air light - en!
sweet Sabbath a - bove; Day nev-er end - ing, all things transcend - ing,

Of the Lord's love on this sweet Sab - bath day.
On the dear Lord's day let glo - ry be shed!
When shall we see him and rest in his love!

REFRAIN.

Beau - ti - ful morn - ing, welcome thy dawn-ing! Day of all oth - ers the

74

BEAUTIFUL MORNING.

bright-est and best; Beau - ti - ful morn - ing, welcome thy dawn - ing!

Hallowed for - ev - er, thy mo - ments are blest.

Rev. W. F. COSNER.

SAFE AT HOME.

[For music, see page 29—"AFTER WHILE."]

1

Ah, this heart shall cease its longing,
Safe at home! safe at home!
Where no anxious cares are thronging,
Safe at home! safe at home!
Now a heavy burden presses,
And I walk through thorny places,
Till my weary wandering ceases,
Safe at home! safe at home!

2

There I'll see no tempest raging,
Safe at home! safe at home!
Sin no warfare wild is waging,
Safe at home! safe at home!
When shall come that blissful waking,
Where no painful head is aching,
Where no throbbing heart is breaking,
Safe at home! safe at home!

3

There are friends who with me parted
Safe at home! safe at home!
No more wandering broken-hearted,
Safe at home! safe at home!
Undisturbed while storms are sweeping,
Calmly now the loved are sleeping,
Ever in their Father's keeping,
Safe at home! safe at home!

4

Dear ones gone before will meet me,
Safe at home! safe at home!
At the pearly gate will greet me,
Safe at home! safe at home!
Saviour, dearest Saviour, hear me!
I am weary: be thou near me!
Oh, sustain me till thou cheer me
Safe at home! safe at home!

CAMP-FIRES OF GOD.

EBEN E. REXFORD.

T. C. O'KANE.

1 Sol - dier of Christ, art thou fam - ished and wea - ry,
2 Is the march wea - ri - some, bear - ing a bur - den?
3 Sol - dier of Je - sus, be brave in eu - dea - vor;

Seems the day long, and the march hard and slow? Ah! there is rest for the
Are bat-tles ma - ny ere con - flict is done? Strive with the faith - ful to
Rest is a - head on the hills o - ver there, Where, in the tents of the

tired and the wea - ry,—Rest which the sol - dier at night - fall shall know.
win heaven's guer - don, Thrill'd by the thought of the rest to be won.
faith - ful, for - ev - er Peace nev - er end - ing the vic - tors shall share.

CHORUS.

Soon, wea - ry sol - dier, the march will be o - ver;

76

CAMP-FIRES OF GOD.

Soon with old comrades sweet rest you shall share; For through the darkness our

eyes can dis-cov-er Camp-fires of God on the hills o-ver there.

LAND OF REST.

A. S. KIEFFER.

1 O land of rest, for thee I sigh; When will the mo-ment come
2 No tran-quil joys on earth I know, No peace-ful shelt'ring dome;
3 To Je-sus Christ I sought for rest; He bade me cease to roam,
4 Wea-ry of wandering round and round This vale of sin and gloom,

When I shall lay my ar-mor by And dwell in peace at home.
This world's a wil-der-ness of woe; This world is not my home.
But fly for suc-cor to his breast,And he'd con-duct me home.
I long to quit th'un-hallowed ground,And dwell with Christ at home.

77

SAILING O'ER LIFE'S SEA. R. A. GLENN.

1 We're a hap - py pil - grim band, Sail - ing to the heavenly land;
2 Though the migh - ty bil - lows swell, They shall nev - er o - ver-whelm;
3 Though, for ma - ny a - ges past, She has braved the storm - y blast,

With a swell - ing sail we on - ward sweep: Though the
Though the break - ers roar up - on the lea; 'Mid the
She's the old Ship Zi - on, as of yore. Safe a-

tem - pest ra - ges long, There is One a - mong the throng
strife His praise will swell, For we've Je - sus at the helm,
mid the rocks and shoals, She has land - ed ma - ny souls

Who will guide the sail - or o'er the deep.
And he'll guide her safe - ly o'er the sea.
Safe at home, on Ca - naan's hap - py shore.

78

SAILING O'ER LIFE'S SEA.

CHORUS.

We are sail - - ing o'er the o - - cean;

We are sail - ing o'er the o - cean; We are sail - ing o'er the o - cean;

We are drift - - - ing with the tide;

We are drift - ing, drift - ing, drift - ing with the tide;

Soon the storms . . . will all be o - - ver;

Soon the storms will all be o'er, Soon the storms will all be o'er,

Soon we'll reach - - - - the oth - er side.

Soon we'll safe - ly reach the oth - er side.

INDEX.

www.ingramcontent.com/pod-product-compliance
Lightning Source LLC
Chambersburg PA
CBHW020252290326
41930CB00039B/1033